CHRISTIE'S

COLLECTABLES

CHRISTIE'S
COLLECTABLES

ART DECO
CERAMICS

Jane Hay

LITTLE, BROWN AND COMPANY
BOSTON NEW YORK LONDON TORONTO

A LITTLE, BROWN BOOK

FIRST PUBLISHED IN GREAT BRITAIN IN 1996
BY LITTLE, BROWN AND COMPANY (UK)

CONCEIVED, EDITED AND DESIGNED BY
MARSHALL EDITIONS
170 PICCADILLY   LONDON W1V 9DD

A CIP catalogue record for this book is available
from the British Library.

ISBN 0-316-87782-4

2 4 6 8 10 9 7 5 3 1

EDITORS HEATHER MAGRILL, ISABELLA RAEBURN
DESIGNERS FRANCES DE REES, HELEN SPENCER
PICTURE EDITOR ELIZABETH LOVING

Marshall Editions would like to thank
Edward Schneider of Christie's Images for his help
in the creation of this book.

Origination by HBM Print Pte, Singapore
Printed and bound in Portugal by Printer Portuguesa

LITTLE, BROWN AND COMPANY (UK)
Brettenham House Lancaster Place London WC2E 7EN

CHRISTIE'S
8 King Street St. James's London SW1Y 6QT

CHRISTIE'S SOUTH KENSINGTON
85 Old Brompton Road London SW7 3LD

CHRISTIE'S
502 Park Avenue New York NY 10022

CHRISTIE'S AUSTRALIA
298 New South Head Road Double Bay Sydney NSW 2028

CHRISTIE'S SOUTH AFRICA
P.O. Box 72126 Parkview Johannesburg 2122

CHRISTIE'S JAPAN
Sankyo Ginza Building 6-5-13 Ginza Chuo-ku Tokyo 104

Contents

PRICE CODES

The following price codes are used in this book:
£A Less than £100 **£B** £101–£300
£C £301–£500 **£D** £501–£1,000 **£E** £1,001–£1,500
£F £1,501–£2,000 **£G** More than £2,000

Valuation is an imprecise art and prices can vary for many
reasons, including the condition of a piece, fashion and national and
regional interest. Prices given in this book are approximate
and based on likely *auction* values. *Insurance* values reflect the
retail replacement price and as such are liable to be higher.

Introduction

$\mathscr{A}$ LIVELY STYLE COMBINING RICH DECORATION WITH geometric outline, Art Deco is properly defined as the style prevalent between the Paris Exhibition of 1925, which introduced the world to "l'Art Décoratif", and the outbreak of World War II, although examples on either side of these limits exist.

$\mathscr{T}$he 1925 Paris Exhibition, officially the "Exposition des Arts Décoratifs et Industriels Modernes", was part of a long tradition of international trade fairs designed to show off the best of modern design to the public and had an enormous impact on contemporary taste. Although it was dominated by the French, it was clear that a new mood was in the air internationally, with the

The pavilion of the Galeries Lafayette at the 1925 Paris Exhibition was one of the most original there.

The interior of the French trans-Atlantic liner
S.S. Normandie *shows Art Deco style at its height.*

organic free-flowing lines of Art Nouveau being replaced by geometric forms and rectilinear designs combined with sumptuous decorative techniques. The style was to reach its apogee a decade later with the launching of the French trans-Atlantic luxury liner S.S. *Normandie* in 1935. Furnished by leading designers, again mostly from France, the ship embodied all that was best in the Art Deco style.

*B*ut the French did not have a monopoly on Art Deco. It was a new look that swept the world, taking many forms and subject to many influences. The development of the film industry did much to popularize the new style. Indeed, there is a whole subsection of Art Deco known as the Odeon style, after the great picture houses of the day which incorporated Sunburst and Egyptianesque motifs with abandon. The advent of the industrial machine age made an impact, as did new

*The ballroom of the Park Lane Hotel, London, shows
typically Art Deco motifs in its decoration.*

forms of travel such as the aeroplane, which gave rise to
dynamic forms associated with speed, notably in Italy
where Futurism took hold.

$\mathscr{O}$ther developments to contribute to the style were the
discovery of Tutankhamun's tomb in 1922 and the
interest of Cubist and Fauvist artists such as Picasso in
African art and sculpture. The emancipation of women,
with their new shorter hairstyles and dresses, as well as
the upsurge of jazz music, can often be seen in figurative
studies from this period. So, too, can the craze for health
that swept Europe after World War I: what can be more
1920s in style than a model of a young woman in a

swimsuit carrying a parasol? Various earlier artists and designers were also extremely influential, among them Charles Rennie Mackintosh, one of the first to take up the rectilinear style, Frank Lloyd Wright, the Bauhaus in Germany and Austria's Wiener Werkstätte.

$\mathcal{T}$he period between the wars was one of immense change, but not all of the new developments were positive. The Wall Street Crash of 1929 heralded the Depression, when people had little money to spend and certainly none for expensive luxury items. This resulted in simple hard-wearing styles which could be made cheaply using the techniques of mass production.

$\mathcal{S}$ince Art Deco ceramics are relatively inexpensive and reflect the tremendous variety of the age – ranging from

William Van Alen's Chrysler Building in New York exploited Art Deco, even in its superb elevators.

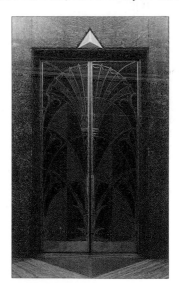

cheap and cheerful to the height of luxury – it is possible to build a varied collection, even on a limited budget, and to derive great enjoyment from doing so.

TIPS FOR COLLECTORS

• Buy what you like and do not allow yourself to be deflected by others. If you become bored with a piece at a later date you can always sell it again, but if you pass up the opportunity to buy something you may find that in years to come you regret it.

• Always buy the best that you can afford, especially with regard to condition. Often a piece that seems costly will gain in value over time and can prove to be an investment. Badly damaged or restored examples,

The fascination with jazz, common in the Art Deco era, is reflected in Clarice Cliff's "Age of Jazz" duo, c.1935.

The carpet of Radio City Music Hall, in the Rockefeller Center, New York, shows images typical of the Jazz Age.

however, will not usually increase in value unless they are exceptionally rare to begin with.

• Take care when cleaning pieces: some decoration is oil based and will come off in detergent; scrubbing can lift off fragile on-glaze enamels; and a rapid change from hot to cold water can result in a nasty crack.

• Keep a record of your purchases. This is useful both for insurance purposes and if you decide to sell in the future. Check with your insurer the value above which pieces should be photographed and separately listed on your insurance.

• Stick to reputable auction houses and dealers. If you can build up a rapport with dealers and auction specialists and they get a feel for your taste, they can look out for pieces which may appeal to you. Only when you have found your feet in your particular field is it time to pit your wits against the car boot sale trader!

Ashtead Pottery I

BASED IN EPSOM, England, Ashtead Pottery was established in 1923 by the philanthropists Sir Lawrence and Kathleen, Lady Weaver, to provide employment for disabled ex-servicemen and their families after World War I. At its height, the pottery persuaded many notable artists to provide designs.

THIS POLYCHROME painted pottery figure of a young girl is entitled "Shy" and was modelled by Phoebe Stabler. A sculptor and designer of some repute, Phoebe was married to Harold Stabler, a director of Poole Pottery, and she sold her designs to several factories. It is also possible to find examples of the same figure produced by Poole Pottery and Royal Doulton, the only variation being in the size and material used.

Height 11½in/29cm £C

Ashtead Pottery II

*THIS BLUE-GLAZED POTTERY LION WAS DESIGNED
by Percy Metcalfe, a well-known sculptor
and stamp designer. Originally made for the 1924
Empire Exhibition at Wembley, London, it was
called the Lion of Industry. It proved so popular that
the "Wembley Lion" was put into general
production and adopted by the Genozo toothpaste
manufacturer for its advertising.*

*ALTHOUGH ASHTEAD POTTERY ENJOYED SOME COMMERCIAL
success in the 1920s, it was unable to survive the
Depression and closed in 1935. Ashtead pieces
are clearly marked with the factory name and often
carry a painted serial number which refers to
the design and the factory order book.*

Height 10in/25cm   £B

Boch Frères 1

AS WITH SO MANY CONTINENTAL EUROPEAN
*potteries, little is known of this Belgian factory, also
called Keramis, because it sustained heavy damage
in World War II and most of its records were
destroyed. What is known is that it was part of
a larger group founded in 1767 at Sept Fontaines in
the Saar region of Germany. In the mid-19th
century, the company split and a new factory was
established at La Louvière in Belgium.*

BOCH FRÈRES WAS MOST FAMOUS FOR ITS EARTHENWARE
*vases, but also had a reputation for using distinctive
decorative techniques and Art Deco shapes and
designs. Its was one of the most important Belgian
contributions to the Art Deco style.*

THIS VASE REFLECTS THE POPULARITY OF GEOMETRIC
*forms, inspired by Cubism and Futurism. Asymmetry
was the new modern look, seeking to escape the
organic style and free-flowing lines of Art Nouveau.*
Height 10in/25cm £C

Boch Frères II

BOTH THE SHAPE AND THE DECORATION OF
this vase are typical of Boch Frères, whose distinctive
wares were first incised with the basic pattern and
then covered with a base coating of a thick
crackle glaze in a neutral colour. The pot was
then enamelled in bold colours within the incised
pattern to create an overall effect that was
reminiscent of Chinese cloisonné.

AS IN THE ART NOUVEAU PERIOD, THE DEPICTION OF
the female form was a popular motif in decorative
ceramics. But on this piece the look has been
transformed from romantic notions of womanhood
to a more geometric and abstract style. Factory
marks are usually a variant of "Keramis" or "Boch
Frères", or a combination of the two.

Height 12in/30cm £D

Burleigh I

Founded in 1877, the Burleigh factory originally specialized in printed tableware. During the 1930s, however, it branched out into hand-painted decorative pieces. Today, the factory is best known for its distinctive range of jugs with modelled handles. Production of this line began in 1931 and continued until the 1950s.

The early models, often designed by Charles Wilkes, had handles shaped as birds or animals. These jugs, with parrot and kingfisher handles, are typical. Since the range was popular and remained in production for a long time, examples are still fairly easy to find and reasonably inexpensive to buy.

Height 9in/23cm   £A (both)

Burleigh II

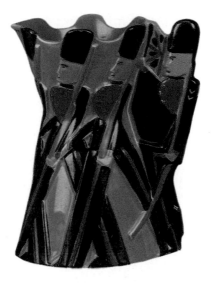

SEVERAL OTHER LINES WERE PRODUCED BY Burleigh, but in smaller quantities. One such range featured human figures on the handle. Sporting subjects, such as cricketers, golfers and tennis players, are often found. More unusual was this type of model, depicting the Changing of the Guard at Buckingham Palace, which came in various palettes. The relative rarity of such jugs means that they tend to command higher prices at auction.

Height 9in/23cm £E

Pre-World War II items commonly carry the factory's distinctive mark, a beehive surrounded by a wreath of leaves.

René Buthaud

*T*RAINED IN FINE ART, *R*ENÉ *B*UTHAUD *(1886–1986)*
turned to ceramics in 1919. He generally worked
in stoneware and was one of the chief exponents of
sgraffito, *a technique that involves dipping a piece*
of one colour into a contrasting slip, then carving
away the slip to reveal the colour beneath.
*B*UTHAUD'S OTHER SPECIALITY WAS HAND-PAINTED FIGURAL
decoration – this scene of Europa and the Bull was
painted directly on the pot. Buthaud favoured
blue-grey or iron red on a stone or cream ground,
and his female figures usually have strong outlines.
His work, which generally bears his painted
signature or initials, is highly collectable,
especially in the U.S. and France.
Height 12½in/32cm   £G

Carlton Ware 1

BASED IN STOKE-ON-TRENT, THE HOME OF
*English pottery, Carlton Ware was a brand name
of Wiltshaw & Robinson. Carlton
produced a wide range of ceramics during
its long history (1890–1992). The output during
the 1920s and '30s included four
distinct areas: moulded tablewares; exotic lustre
wares; geometric shaped pieces known as the
Moderne range; and those with brightly
coloured stylized designs.*

PIECES OF TABLEWARE DECORATED WITH EMBOSSED,
*or relief-moulded, flowers, vegetables and fruit
were a particular speciality of the factory, as were
small and novelty items made out of leaves.
This salad bowl with lobster-claw feet is typical.
It is from the popular Salad Ware range and takes
the form of lettuce leaves with tomatoes.
Since such pieces were made in large numbers they
are, at present, less collectable than
some of Carlton's other wares.*

Diameter 12in/30cm £A

Carlton Ware II

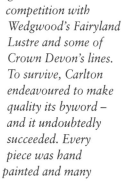

CARLTON WARE'S LUXURY ranges were in direct competition with Wedgwood's Fairyland Lustre and some of Crown Devon's lines. To survive, Carlton endeavoured to make quality its byword – and it undoubtedly succeeded. Every piece was hand painted and many were embellished with gilding, although little is known of the individuals who produced them.

THIS BISCUIT BOX, A TYPICAL EXAMPLE, WAS DECORATED with the "Egyptian Fan" design. The pattern is simply one example of the influence that the discovery of Tutankhamun's tomb in 1922 had on popular culture. The name "Egyptian Fan" was one of those given to patterns by recent collectors to help them identify different designs. This was necessary because, although every item was marked on the base with a pattern number, no official names existed.

Height 5½in/14cm   £B

Pieces from the Art Deco period usually have a transfer-printed factory mark in script on the base. Any numbers painted alongside the mark denote the serial number of the design.

Carlton Ware III

IN ADDITION TO MAKING TRADITIONAL WARES, Carlton's designers embraced the modern era, as can be seen in this magnificent "Moderne" tea set, with its attractive matt grey glaze and gilt handles. Legend has it that a French designer sought refuge in England during World War II and briefly worked at the factory, leaving behind this avant-garde shape, but no records exist to confirm the story.

Height coffee pot 8in/20cm Set £B

TO THE LEFT OF THE TEA SET ARE TWO OTHER PIECES WITH the brightly coloured and stylized designs typical of Carlton. The jug features the "Tiger Tree" design; the ginger jar and cover display the "Sunburst" pattern.

Height both 8in/20cm £B (jug); £C (jar)

Clarice Cliff I

ONE OF THE DOMINANT DESIGNERS OF THE
*Art Deco period, Clarice Cliff (1899–1972) started
out at A.J. Wilkinson's Royal Staffordshire
Pottery in Burslem, where she fell in love with the
factory boss, Colley Shorter. With his guidance, she
underwent a long period of training, which
included regular visits to Paris and London to see
what was at the forefront of modern design.*
IN 1927 SHE WAS GIVEN HER OWN STUDIO AND ASSISTANTS
*at another Wilkinson factory, the Newport
Pottery, and was extremely successful between the
wars. Cliff designed both the shape and decoration of
her wares, which were then hand-copied by her
team. Part of her talent lay in taking
sophisticated avant-garde designs from Europe and
reworking them for the British market.
This single-handled Lotus pitcher is decorated in the
"Blue W" pattern, using the classic colors that
Cliff employed for almost all her designs.*
Height 12in/30cm £G

Clarice Cliff II

CLIFF BEGAN HER CAREER WITH SIMPLE GEOMETRIC
*designs, now commonly known as "Original Bizarre"
because the factory mark has the "Bizarre" trade
name. Later she progressed to more exciting abstract
designs inspired by the French Cubists.*

IN ADDITION TO GEOMETRIC PATTERNS, SHE DESIGNED
*lines featuring stylized landscapes. Commercially,
they were more successful than the abstract patterns,
and many survive. These bright scenes brought
cheer to people in the Depression and were
favored as wedding presents.*

PIECES IN UNUSUAL SHAPES, SUCH AS CONICAL SUGAR
*sifters, are particularly popular with collectors.
This one features a typical landscape design
known as "House and Bridge." Behind is a baluster
vase in the "Oranges" pattern and to the right
a small vase in the "Orange Roof Cottage" design.
The beaker in the foreground is decorated with
the classic abstract pattern "Tennis."*

Height large vase 8½in/22cm   £D (all)

Clarice Cliff III

*DURING THE EARLY 1930S,
Clarice Cliff became
involved with the
Harrods Exhibition,
for which many
artists of the day
turned their talents to
designing tableware.
Her studio at
Wilkinson's produced
the pottery, while the
china and glasswares
were made elsewhere.*

*FOLLOWING THE DEATH OF HIS INVALID WIFE,
Colley Shorter finally married Cliff in 1940. With
a happy marriage and the factory restricted to
making utility ware during World War II, Cliff went
into semi-retirement, which
later became permanent.
She has left a legacy of
designs which still
appeal today.
THE TOP PLATE
is decorated in the
"Sunray" pattern,
which is said to have
been inspired by the
skyscrapers of New
York. Many collectors
call this design "Night and
Day," after the Cole Porter
song. The lower plate features another classic
abstract design known as "Lightning."*

Diameter both 8in/20cm £D

Clarice Cliff IV

THE POPULARITY OF CLARICE CLIFF'S WORK
*means that fakes abound. Although these two
examples of the "Orange Roof Cottage" pattern
look similar, the pitcher on the right is a fake. It may
seem genuine, but important differences
become obvious when it is next to the original.
The windows of the cottage have reflections;
the bridge is misdrawn; and the color scheme
is wrong: the orange banding in the copy is too bright
and red. (Many of the original, more muted, enamel
colors are toxic and so are now unavailable.)
A convincing factory mark is no guarantee of
authenticity either, since good replicas exist.*
Height left 9in/23cm £E; right 12in/30cm

Cliff marks are distinctive.
In the years 1929–39, they
were put on in black either
with a rubber stamp or with
a simple lithograph over the
glaze. They usually include
the range name, such as
"Bizarre", within the mark.

Susie Cooper 1

Born in 1902, Susie Cooper was a contemporary of Clarice Cliff, but outlived her more successful rival. She began her career at A.E. Gray & Co. Ltd. in 1922 and was soon given her own designer backstamp. During her seven years at Gray's, Cooper became involved in lustre decoration, only later moving on to more abstract Cubist designs. Of her many different design periods, only the Cubist bears comparison with the work of Clarice Cliff. This vase, decorated with the "Moon and Mountain" pattern, is typical of Cooper's output at that time.

Height 8in/20cm £D

Susie Cooper's distinctive backstamp while at Gray's consisted of the liner mark of Gray's pottery with the legend "Designed by Susie Cooper" below.

Susie Cooper II

ONE OF SUSIE COOPER'S MOST FAMOUS SHAPES
*was that of the "Kestrel" range, introduced at the
British Industries Fair in 1932. The distinctive
design, shown here in the form of a coffee pot, is set
off by the decoration, obviously inspired by
the abstract artist Piet Mondrian.*

COOPER EXPERIENCED PROBLEMS WITH HER EARLY
*on-glaze decoration, and many examples of her
work from this period are in poor repair. She
had particular trouble with
oxidizing or flaking enamels,
a problem Clarice Cliff
also encountered but
overcame sooner.*

Height 10in/25cm £C (pot)

Susie Cooper III

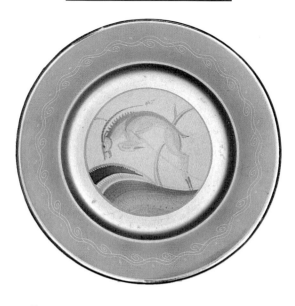

*In 1930 Susie Cooper began designing and
producing her own wares. One of her independent
ventures was at Wood & Son's Crown Works in
Burslem, in The Potteries. This animal plate – typical
of her output at the time – has been delicately hand
painted in the centre and enhanced with silver
lustre. It also shows one of Cooper's later favourite
techniques,* sgraffito *decoration, around the rim.*

Diameter 8in/20cm £D

*Susie Cooper was at the forefront of Modernism
and favoured modern industrial techniques to
produce tableware that was easy to use and maintain.
In later years, she took up the new lithographed
decorative techniques suitable for mass production.
After a long and varied career, she went to work
for Wedgwood after World War II.*

Susie Cooper IV

TOWARD THE END OF THE **A**RT **D**ECO PERIOD,
*Susie Cooper produced a range of studio wares with
a more handmade feel. This example, which is
signed, is from the "Carved Ware" range which
features simple forms incised with animal designs.*
Height 12in/30cm £B

Susie Cooper's
later pieces bear
her distinctive flowing
signature incised
on the base.

Crown Devon I

Like Carlton Ware, Crown Devon produced a full range of table and fancy wares, and was based near Stoke-on-Trent. Indeed, the two firms were direct rivals and many of their goods, in particular the lustre wares, are virtually indistinguishable. This can be explained by the fact that two of the leading lights at Carlton, Enoch Wood and George Barker, defected to Crown Devon in 1930 as decorating manager and sales director respectively.

This vase is typical of Crown Devon's lustre-decorated pieces. The glossy blue ground is enamelled in colours and gilt with an outlandish floral pattern.

Height 6¾in/17cm £B

Crown Devon is clearly printed "Fielding's", representing S. Fielding & Co., of which Crown Devon was the brand name.

Crown Devon II

*T*HE CROSS-FERTILIZATION OF IDEAS BETWEEN
*Carlton and Crown Devon was not unusual in this
period: market share was vital at a time of limited
sales, and companies regularly took good ideas from
various sources and developed them further. Crown
Devon competed in the market for Goldscheider- and
Katzhütte-type pottery figures, for example,
ruthlessly copying successful models.*

*T*HIS VASE FROM THE MATT-DECORATED RANGE SHOWS
*strong enamel colour and delicate gilding. The
spider's web was a popular motif in the Art Deco
period because of its strong geometric qualities.*

Height 6¾in/17cm £B

French porcelain 1

IN EUROPE, ONE OF THE MORE POPULAR ART DECO
figural pieces was the luminaire, *or night light, which
provided the subtle lighting considered essential
for creating the right atmosphere in the home. Since
porcelain becomes translucent when fired, it is
perfect for night lights – no other ceramic
material allows light to filter through.*

MANY NIGHT LIGHT SHAPES WERE INSPIRED BY THE POPULAR
*culture of the day. This typical example by Delblaize
depicts Harlequin and Columbine from the
Commedia dell'Arte plays. Nothing is known of
the artist, who simply signed his name on the piece.
This is not an uncommon phenomenon, since
factories often sold undecorated items to artists and
then re-fired the painted articles in their kiln.*

Height 11in/28cm £D

French porcelain II

Following a tradition of about 200 years of manufacture by such leading factories as Sèvres and Limoges, French Art Deco porcelain was of the highest quality. These exquisitely decorated plates are part of a service of 18, each signed "G. Nielz, Delveaux". No information exists on either artist or manufacturer – Delveaux may have been the retailer's mark or the trade name for a larger manufacturer.

Made for the luxury end of the market, each plate is painted in brilliant colours, both under and over the glaze. The subject, scenes of marine life, was popular in France at the time, since biologist Jacques Cousteau had recently invented the aqualung, enabling study of life under the sea.

Diameter 8in/20cm £E

German pottery

ALTHOUGH GERMANY produced some first-class porcelain and was famous for factories such as Rosenthal and Meissen, stoneware and pottery were favoured at the more popular end of the market because they tended to be less expensive to produce.

THIS POTTERY PIECE is typical of German figural works of the period. They almost always feature young women in evening gowns or other slightly risqué clothing, often leading a terrier or exotic borzoi hound. This model is wearing a sunsuit with lounging pyjamas – then the height of fashion. Since the piece was made for export, the base is simply marked "Germany".

Height 9½in/24cm £C

German stoneware

THIS STONEWARE GROUP, BASED ON GREEK MYTH,
depicts Neptune, rather improbably dressed in what
looks like a fireman's helmet and waterproof
trousers, astride a hippocampus, or sea horse.
THE HEAVY CRACKLED GLAZE HAS BEEN SUBTLY PAINTED IN
shades of blue and green and given a second firing.
Unlike the figure opposite, which was mass produced,
this piece – with its high-quality composition
and execution – was almost certainly the work of an
artist: the absence of a factory mark suggests
that it came from a small studio working either
within a larger factory or independently.
Height 14in/36cm £E

Ginori

ORIGINALLY KNOWN AS THE DOCCIA FACTORY,
*Ginori was founded near Florence in 1737 by Carlo
Ginori, who brought the secret of porcelain
manufacture from Vienna. During the late 19th
century it was adapted for mass production, and in
1896 it amalgamated with another factory
to become Richard-Ginori, although it is now
commonly known simply as Ginori.*

BETWEEN 1923 AND 1938 IT EMPLOYED THE NOW FAMOUS
*Italian architect and designer Gio Ponti to revitalize
its output. Although he was avant-garde, he also
liked to rework traditional shapes and motifs. This
porcelain box and cover decorated with silver lustre,
entitled "Balletto", is typical of his work. The
stylized figures are mounted on a conventional fluted
oval form decorated with sprays of foliage.*

Height 9in/23cm £F

Goldscheider 1

ONE OF THE LARGEST
*Austrian ceramics manufacturers of the Art Deco
era, the Goldscheider factory had a thriving export
business. Polychrome pottery figures, often designed
by outside artists, formed much of its output.
They tend to be fragile and may crack at weaker
points such as the wrists and ankles.*
THE LEFT AND CENTRAL FIGURES HERE ARE BY THE AUSTRIAN
*sculptor Stefan Dakon, who also worked in
bronze and ivory. As well as the factory mark these
hand-painted pieces bear Dakon's signature. The
piece on the right is unsigned but is typical of Josef
Lorenzl, who also often worked for the firm.*
Height left 4½in/11cm   £E (centre); £D (others)

Goldscheider II

DURING THE **A**RT **D**ECO period, Goldscheider also specialized in terracotta wall masks. With their stylized lines and primary colours, they owe much to the work of the Austrian Modernist group, the Wiener Werkstätte. Only a few models were made, but they were hand painted in numerous colour schemes.

SINCE TERRACOTTA IS delicate, porous and easily damaged, examples in perfect condition are now rare. The coiled hair tends to crack first.

FROM THE LATE 1930S GOLDSCHEIDER PIECES WERE made in Staffordshire by Myott, Son & Co. Similar masks were also made in central Europe, although those made there since 1945 are easy to identify – they are marked only with their country of origin and tend to be less well made.

Height 11in/28cm £C

Goldscheider wares have a thick crackled glaze and distinctive factory mark. Earlier models were often marked "Wien" (Vienna) while later models made for export were marked "Made in Austria".

Carruthers Gould

PRODUCED AT THE WILKINSON FACTORY,
*these pottery Toby jugs were based on designs by
the famous political cartoonist Sir Francis
Carruthers Gould (1844–1920). Although not Art
Deco in the strict sense of the word, they are typical
of the patriotic commemorative pieces produced
in Britain between the wars and
depict figures such as Lloyd George and Lord
Kitchener. Commemorative wares celebrating Allied
successes in World War I were vital in boosting
morale during the Depression.*
Height 10in/25cm £G

Geneviève Granger

ONE OF THE FEW COMMERCIALLY SUCCESSFUL
*female sculptors of the time, this French-born artist
produced works in terracotta, bronze, ivory
and pottery. She was well known and showed at the
Paris Exhibition of 1925 – commonly seen as
heralding the start of the Art Deco period.*
MOST OF HER MODELS WERE FIRST MADE IN BRONZE AT THE
*Etling foundry and only then passed to the ceramics
manufacturer. They usually carry a triangular
impressed factory mark, "Editions Etling", and a
facsimile signature. This pottery model of a naked
woman, with its simple lines and low-key decoration,
is typical of her work. It has a crackle glaze with
blue sponged painting to the head and base.*
Height 15in/38cm   £D

Gustavsberg

Dᴜʀɪɴɢ ᴛʜᴇ Aʀᴛ Dᴇᴄᴏ ᴘᴇʀɪᴏᴅ, Gᴜsᴛᴀᴠsʙᴇʀɢ,
*one of Sweden's oldest ceramics factories, was at
the forefront of Scandinavian Modernism. The
driving force behind the factory was its
artistic director, Wilhem Kåge, who worked
there between 1917 and 1950.*

"Aʀɢᴇɴᴛᴀ" ᴡᴀʀᴇ, ɪɴᴛʀᴏᴅᴜᴄᴇᴅ ʙʏ Kåɢᴇ ɪɴ 1930, ᴡᴀs
*one of Gustavsberg's most famous ranges.
Usually glazed in matt green or a deep mottled
burgundy, it had rich silver inlay. This charger is
decorated with mermaids, a motif popular then, and
the glaze has been applied to simulate bubbles.
Pieces from the range are usually fully marked in
silver and carry the pattern number.*
Diameter 18in/46cm £D

Harrods Exhibition 1

HELD AT London's famous department store in 1934, the Harrods exhibition was the brainchild of painter Graham Sutherland, designer Milner Gray and manufacturer Thomas Acland Fennemore, director of E. Brain & Co. Its purpose was to produce a series of designs, both on ceramics and on glass, which would show that it was possible to unite artists and industry and make modern art accessible to the average person.

A LEADING LIGHT OF THE BLOOMSBURY GROUP, VANESSA BELL (1879–1961) was one of 28 artists and designers invited to submit ideas for tableware. These pieces are from a complete dinner service, entitled "Vanessa", produced in Clarice Cliff's workshops at Wilkinson's. Each one was painted freehand in blue enamel on an opaque white glaze and has a band of brown dots around the rim.

Diameter plates 8in/20cm   £E–£G

Harrods Exhibition II

THREE SITES WERE USED FOR PRODUCING EXHIBITION *wares: A.J. Wilkinson's for the pottery; E. Brain & Co. (also known as Foley China) for the bone china; and Stuart Glass. Just 12 services were made of each design and were marked "First edition" on the reverse; the most popular later went into large-scale production. Many of the designs submitted were unsuitable – they were impractical either as tableware or for mass production. But enough exhibition ware exists today to make it a worthwhile collecting field in its own right.*

DAME LAURA KNIGHT (1877–1970) WAS ONE OF *the most commercially successful British artists of the era and contributed several designs to the exhibition. This tea service, entitled "Cupid", was made at Foley China. Its printed outline is enamelled in black and green. Since the black enamel tends to lift and flake off, care must be taken when handling pieces.*
Height cup 1½in/4cm   £D–£F

Harrods Exhibition III

IMAGES OF CIRCUS LIFE WERE A *favoured motif for Laura Knight. Her "Circus" series, produced by Clarice Cliff at Wilkinson's, is the best known and most sought after today. Part of its popularity may be due to the fact that Knight, unlike the other artists, also designed the shapes for her extensive service. All the items, from tureens to jugs and bowls, had finials and legs modelled as intertwined clowns.*

THIS TABLE LAMP, ONE OF ONLY *three known to exist, matches the rest of the service and represents the apogee of the style. The column of intertwined circus folk is enamelled in bright colours embellished with gilt. The top is painted with swags reminiscent of the top of a marquee – a motif repeated across the service, especially as an edging on plates. An underglaze pink transfer print was the starting point for applying the decoration, which was then enamelled free-hand on glaze.*

Height 19in/48cm   £G

Harrods Exhibition IV

THIS PLATE WAS ONE OF THE FOLEY-PRODUCED *range of Laura Knight designs. The whole pattern is painted freehand in colours and purple lustre and appears to represent Adam and Eve in the Garden of Eden, although the exact title is unknown. The theme does, however, fit in with another of Knight's patterns for Foley, which is entitled "Dove" and depicts scenes after the Flood.*

PERHAPS BECAUSE THE COMPOSITION IS RELATIVELY *weak and the lustre prone to wear, this was the least produced of Laura Knight's designs and examples of it are hardest to find.*

Diameter 8in/20cm   £D

Harrods Exhibition v

THIS HIGHLY SUCCESSFUL PATTERN BY
*Ernest Proctor (1885–1935) was produced at
Wilkinson's on green-glazed pottery. It was painted
freehand in silver lustre in Clarice Cliff's studio.
Proctor's wife Dod also designed for the exhibition.*
Diameter 8in/20cm £B

IT IS NOT KNOWN HOW MANY EXHIBITION DESIGNS
*were put into production, but each piece is clearly
marked on the reverse with a printed factory
backstamp and the artist's signature. In addition to
the artists featured here, others whose work was
produced include: John Armstrong, Freda Beardmore,
Angelica Bell, Frank Brangwyn, Eva Crofts, John
Everett, Gordon Forsyth, Moira Forsyth, Duncan
Grant, Milner Gray, Barbara Hepworth, Paul Nash,
Ben Nicholson, Albert Rutherston, Graham
Sutherland, Allan Walton and Michael Wellmer.*

Harrods Exhibition VI

BILLY WATERS (1896–1979) SPENT FIVE YEARS AT *Newlyn, Cornwall, where she studied under Ernest Proctor. Today she is best known for the quality of her designs. This soup bowl and stand are part of a dinner service produced at Wilkinson's. Printed and painted in greys, greens and blacks on pottery, this highly successful design could be easily adapted for tableware shapes and lent itself to industrial production. The service is even durable enough to withstand modern use.*

THE LEAPING DEER IS A COMMON MOTIF ON 1930S DESIGNS. *Susie Cooper used it on her factory backstamp when her studio was at the Crown Works, Burslem. It was also used at Poole Pottery, incorporated into delicately scrolling foliage, where it proved so successful that the design is still in production today.*

Diameter bowl 4¼in/11cm £B

Katzhütte Thuringia

*D*ECORATIVE EARTHENWARE *figures produced for the lower end of the market were the speciality of this small factory. Thuringia, one of the centres of the German ceramics industry, played host to many small factories, much like Limoges in France.*

*K*ATZHÜTTE'S CHARMING *figures capture the spirit of the day. They often feature film stars, since this was the age when films first caught the public imagination. There are also sporting subjects, since in prewar Germany it was considered both fashionable and beneficial to be healthy.*

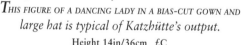

*T*HIS FIGURE OF A DANCING LADY IN A BIAS-CUT GOWN AND *large hat is typical of Katzhütte's output.*

Height 14in/36cm £C

The highly distinctive factory mark takes the form of a pictogram. Katzhütte literally means "cat's house", so the mark shows a cat, with the letter H above it, inside a house.

Robert Lallement

A well-known French ceramics designer, Robert Lallement (1902–54) caught the flavour of the Art Deco period. After initial training at Lachenal, a large pottery manufacturer in Paris, he set up his own small enterprise in that city.

The majority of his pieces are simple geometric forms, usually vases, on which his own designs are painted. These examples are typical: the square vase on the left is painted with scenes of Chopin playing to an attentive audience; on the right is a bowed rectangular vase painted with the popular Art Deco motif of a browsing deer. Although the pottery itself is quite fragile, the decoration is applied with assurance and style. Most pieces are signed in black with "Lallement" in capital letters or script.

Height left 8in/20cm £D; right 5in/13cm £C

Lenci 1

Established in Turin in 1919, the Lenci factory was at the forefront of Italian Art Deco. Its output was considerable and included much that catered for the religious tastes of the home market, such as Madonna and Child groups and wall masks of modest ladies. Although best known for its figures, Lenci also made decorative tableware which, until 1939, was painted with Cubist designs.

This group, entitled "Mamma Sirena", was designed in 1935 by Helen König Scavini, one of Lenci's top designers. It is a fantasy representation of motherhood – a common theme – and uses matt and shiny glazes, a feature of many Lenci pieces.

Height 14in/36cm £G

Lenci II

THIS SHINY-GLAZED Betty Grable-style figure, attributed to Lenci, was designed by an unknown artist. Such figures of immodestly dressed women were popular with the designers, but did not sell in large numbers and are now hard to find, although they are favoured by today's collectors. IN THE 1930s, figures of women in contemporary fashion were preferred to nudes.

Height 13in/33cm £E

Lenci factory marks are usually hand painted in black on the base. They are often dated and sometimes carry an artist's insignia, although many designers remained anonymous. The "Made in Italy" mark shows that this piece was destined for export. Occasionally it is possible to find a piece's original paper label.

Limoges

FINE CERAMICS HAVE BEEN MADE IN the city of Limoges, France, since the 17th century, but it is only since the 1870s that they have been mass produced. As in Thuringia, Germany, many small companies traded under the Limoges name, among them Serpaut, which made this piece.

PORCELAIN NIGHT lights such as this were essential in the 1920s and '30s home. The Egyptian style, sparked by the discovery of Tutankhamun's tomb in 1922, is evident in the design of a high priestess holding sacrificial bowls. Priestesses were a popular motif and can be seen in much of the decorative art of the period.

Height 6¾in/17cm   £C

The Limoges mark from this period is quite distinctive. As well as the mark shown here, pieces usually carried pattern and factory names.

Longwy

*THE CERAMICISTS AT THE FRENCH FACTORY LONGWY
used the same technique as Boch Frères to make this
pottery plate. The cloisonné effect, which imitates
Persian patterns, was developed in the Bordeaux
region by artists such as Theodor Deck, but became
popular with many manufacturers.*

*MADE FOR THE FRENCH DESIGN STUDIO PRIMAVERA, PART OF
the Paris department store Au Printemps, this piece
has enamelled decoration and features a jungle
landscape with naked women. It was inspired by the
recent interest of artists such as Picasso in
African art. The piece is stamped "Primavera
Longwy France" on the base.*

Diameter 14½in/37cm £E

Moorcroft

WILLIAM MOORCROFT (1872–1945) LEARNED HIS
*trade at James Macintyre & Co. in Staffordshire
before setting up his own company in 1913. The
pottery is distinctive because the outlines of
the designs – commonly flowers, fungi or landscapes –
are made using a kind of tube-lining technique.
This magnificent vase, dated 1928, is decorated with
a combination of two well-known patterns,
"Eventide" and "Moonlit Blue".*

IT IS MARKED WITH AN IMPRESSED "MOORCROFT" AND THE
*painted initials "W.M.", which between the wars
were generally blue. The factory remains in family
hands and is still true to its founder's style.*

Height 18½in/47cm £G

Keith Murray

THIS NEW ZEALAND-BORN DESIGNER (1892–1981) worked on a freelance basis at Wedgwood from 1933 to 1946 while waiting to find a suitable position in his chosen profession of architecture. He designed a series of pots and tableware which had a great impact. His style was a precursor of the fashion for simplicity which informed British design after 1945, and his shapes were produced at Wedgwood into the 1950s.

MURRAY'S DESIGNS WERE MADE EITHER IN earthenware or in the black and brown basalt for which Wedgwood is famous. Often they were moulded, but the basalt pieces at the top of the range had linear decoration carved in the body. The earthenware pieces were covered in matt coloured glazes designed for the range. The black basalt wares – signed on the bottom in red – are his rarest.

Diameter vase 10in/25cm   £B; £D (bowl)

Prewar pieces are easily identified by the full printed signature, like this one, in the backstamp. It is usually beneath the glaze and can be in any colour. Items made after 1941 were simply marked "K.M.".

Keith Murray
WEDGWOOD
MADE IN ENGLAND

Poole Pottery 1

FOUNDED IN THE 1870S AS A TILE MANUFACTURER,
Poole Pottery became a partnership between the
original owner Cyril Carter, John Adams and Harold
Stabler; it was finally named after the Dorset
town where it is still based. Adams was responsible
for new shapes and glazes, while Carter's wife
Truda designed the patterns, and Phoebe and
Harold Stabler the sculptural pieces.
THIS IMPRESSIVE VASE, MADE BETWEEN 1929 AND 1934,
was designed by Truda Carter and decorated by Ann
Hatchard, a senior painter. Its black ground
is unusual, but its dense stylized foliage is typical.
Height 19in/48cm £G

Poole Pottery II

*P*OOLE *P*OTTERY WARE *IS* TYPIFIED *BY A* CREAMY
*crackle glaze over red earthenware pottery,
which was painted in muted pastel shades with
dense floral, animal and bird designs.
After a while the source for the red earthenware
dried up, but the company continued with
ordinary white pottery, dipped in red slip, which
was covered in a creamy or grey crackle glaze.
This is why a distinctive ring is often found
on the base of the pot: when the factory
mark was impressed into the clay it left a ring
of white around the central mark.*
*T*HIS PLATE IS DECORATED WITH A DESIGN BY *T*RUDA *C*ARTER,
*adapted from a Harold Stabler faience panel
design. The design was converted to a mosaic floor
for the 1928 Building Trades Exhibition.*
Diameter 16in/40cm £D

Charlotte Rhead 1

CHARLOTTE RHEAD (1885–1947) WAS THE THIRD generation of a family of Staffordshire potters. These pieces are typical of her work – pottery with tube-lining decoration. The jug at the back is in the "Palermo" pattern, produced from c.1932 and one of her more Art Deco style designs. Of the other pieces, only those centre back and bottom right have a pattern name – "Wisteria".

Height "Palermo" jug 8in/20cm £B (all)

Charlotte Rhead II

THIS PLAQUE IS POSSIBLY THE RAREST EXAMPLE OF Charlotte Rhead's work known. It is a reworking of one of the earliest patterns that she produced, in 1915 when she was working for Wood & Sons, and shows Japanese scenes, which had become popular in the Art Nouveau period and remained so until the outbreak of World War II.

Diameter 12in/30cm £G

Charlotte Rhead often wrote the "C" of her signature as an "L" with a long underline since she preferred to be known as Lottie. The number is that of the pattern.

Rosenthal

Founded in 1879 in Bavaria, the Rosenthal
factory established itself before the end of the century,
producing high-quality bone china tableware in the
Art Nouveau style. The factory remained at
the forefront of current styles and even today
collaborates with contemporary artists to produce
lithographed limited edition plates.
In the 1920s and '30s it made many Art Deco figures
and groups in porcelain, with either a pale cream or
clear glaze. This bust, with its stylized form and
angular lines, is typical. Factory marks are usually
underglaze transfer printed in green, and the incised
artist's insignia is often on the body.
Height 19in/48cm £D

Royal Copenhagen

*ESTABLISHED IN 1873,
this factory is the
major ceramics
producer in
Denmark and
is endorsed by
the Danish
royal family.
Today it is well
known for its
reproductions of
old tableware patterns
and for its porcelain
figurines, painted
in shades
of mushroom
and blue.*

*THIS DISTINCTIVE GREY
stoneware figure, with its
mottled brown glaze, is
a departure from the
factory's standard
work and was one of
a group of stoneware
figures, mostly of animal subjects. It was originally
modelled in the early 1930s and was probably
designed by Knud Khyn (1880–1969), who
was responsible for the series.*

*IT REPRESENTS HARVEST, WITH A NUDE WOMAN
standing before sheaves of wheat. All Royal
Copenhagen ceramics are clearly marked
in underglaze blue, usually with three wavy lines
and the serial number of the model.*

Height 19¼in/49cm £C

Royal Doulton 1

FOUNDED IN 1815, ROYAL Doulton has been making figurines since c.1913, and in that time more than 2,000 models have appeared. One of the best-known figurine designers was Leslie Harradine (1887–1965). In the late 1920s, he made several figures of flappers, bathers and so forth. Most of these were in production for only a short period because they were deemed too risqué.

FIGURE H.N. 1204, MADE FROM 1925 to 1940, is typical, with her music hall artiste dress and fan. Originally called "Fanny", she was renamed "Angela", but even this more decorous name did not keep her in production.

Height 7¼in/18.5cm   £D

Royal Doulton figures are usually catalogued by their "H.N." number, referring to Harry Nixon, who was largely responsible for starting the figurine range. Originally they had a printed factory mark with the name and H.N. number painted, usually in green or black, but now the whole mark is printed.

Royal Doulton II

*"*CHORUS GIRL*", H.N. 1401, WAS ONE OF the many figurines modelled by Leslie Harradine and was produced from 1930 to 1936. Originally launched in 1923 as "Harlequinade", a slightly more demure model, she was intended to depict Columbine from the Commedia dell'Arte plays and was one of Royal Doulton's first ladies to sport the new shorter-length dress. "Harlequinade" was taken out of production shortly after the introduction of "Chorus Girl".*

Height 8½in/21.5cm £D

*"*THE PRINCE OF WALES*", H.N. 1217, AGAIN modelled by Harradine, was produced from 1926 to 1938. This time it was not deference to social mores that caused the figure to be withdrawn but Edward VIII's abdication to marry Mrs. Simpson in 1936. Based on a portrait by Sir Alfred Munnings, it was sold for two years after the abdication, perhaps because Edward was still so popular.*

Height 7¼in/18.5cm £D

*"*BILLY BUNNIKINS*" COMES FROM A SERIES OF nursery ware designed in the 1930s by Barbara Vernon, also known as Sister Mary Barbara, daughter of the general manager of Doulton's at the time. The original Bunnikins figures (six in all) were produced for only a few years from 1938 and were withdrawn in World War II.*

Height 4in/10cm £D

Sèvres I

THE FRENCH FACTORY SÈVRES IS MOST FAMOUS FOR *its 18th-century porcelain. But the Art Deco pieces produced in the 1920s and '30s, when Sèvres had the best-known contemporary artists and designers working for it, are also exquisite.*
DESIGNED BY JACQUES-EMILE RUHLMANN (1879–1933), *this bronze-mounted porcelain vase was decorated by Adrien-August Leduc. Ruhlmann, one of the foremost exponents of the Art Deco style, is best known for his furniture. The subtlety of this abstract design is typical of the period, but its superb quality could only be by Sèvres. The vase is signed "A. Leduc" and is dated 1931. It also bears a paper label inscribed "18-2 2.050-Ruhlmann-Leduc".*
Height 8½in/22cm £G

Sèvres II

JEAN **M**AYODON *(1893–1967) worked for many years at the Sèvres factory and eventually became its artistic director in 1941–42. Among his artistic endeavours are several important commissions for the luxury liner S.S. Normandie, launched in 1935 and famous for its interior decor in the Art Deco style.* **M**AYODON WAS A KEEN *experimentalist in glazing and firing techniques, as can be seen on this vase, which is decorated with the "net of gold" technique for which he is best known. He is also identified with Classical Greek subject matter evidenced by this composition of mythological figures. In this instance the base is marked with the artist's monogram, although not all of his works are signed.*

Height 12in/30cm £G

Shelley I

THE SHELLEY WORKS (1910–66) DEVELOPED FROM
the Staffordshire company Foley Wileman, founded
in the late 19th century. Although best known for
its Art Deco bone china tea sets, Shelley extended the
range into dinner services, the larger pieces of which
were made of a more durable heat-resistant
ceramic than that used for cups and saucers.

FROM THE "VOGUE" RANGE, THIS SELECTION OF DINNER WARE
uses an overlapping rectangle motif, simply
printed and enamelled in black and orange, and is
typical of patterns of this period.

Width platter 15in/38cm   Service £D

THE FACTORY MARK, REGISTERED IN 1910, IS A SIMPLE SHIELD
enclosing the word "Shelley". The painted serial
numbers accompanying the factory mark refer to the
date when the design was introduced, and the letter
prefixing the number refers to the cup shape.

Shelley II

THIS CERAMIC MODEL, typically dressed in the clothes of the era, right down to the cloche hat, is the famous "Shelley Girl" designed in the mid-1920s purely for advertising purposes. Intended for use in shop displays, she was part of a concerted advertising campaign, which included posters and magazines, to persuade the public that tea drinking was sophisticated and fashionable.

ALTHOUGH SHE BEGAN LIFE without a name, she came to be called Elsie Harding when the company had to invent a character for her because she was so well known. At one point painters from the factory were given the same style distinctive paisley patterned dress to wear when they were doing demonstrations in department stores. But Elsie Harding's fame was short-lived and she disappeared from the advertising campaigns in 1930.

Height 10in/25cm   £D

Shelley III

THESE TRIOS OF CUP, saucer and plate show three of the best-known shapes used in the bone china tea services of the Art Deco era. In most instances, the teapot was an optional extra which was not sold as part of the service.

"VOGUE" (TOP) WAS designed by Shelley's foremost designer, Eric Slater, and introduced in 1930. It is very modern, but the cup is difficult to hold because the triangular handle is solid.

"REGENT" (CENTRE) WAS introduced in 1932 and proved to be enduringly popular, perhaps because the form, while stylish, was not too extreme and was also functional.

THE SLIGHTLY OLDER "Queen Anne" style (bottom) came on to the market in 1926. All the trios have side plates in the "Queen Anne" shape.

Width plates 4½in/11.5cm £A

John Skeaping

ACTIVE AS A SCULPTOR IN ENGLAND IN THE 1920s and '30s, Skeaping (1901–80) designed a series of animal figures for Wedgwood, for which he was paid a total of £100. At the time, the effects of the Depression were reducing the factory's profits, so it was trying to move away from exclusive high-quality wares toward simpler, less costly designs.

SKEAPING DESIGNED 14 ANIMAL STUDIES, 10 OF WHICH went into mass production. The figures were made in various bodies and glazes, including basalt. This is the "Polar Bear" model, covered in "Moonstone" glaze. The other production models were: "Buffalo", "Tiger and Buck", "Duiker" (a type of antelope) standing and sitting, "Fallow Deer", "Monkeys", "Sea Lion", "Bison" and "Kangaroo". They usually have an impressed signature on the top of the base, but it can be hard to see if the glaze is thick.

Height 7in/18cm   £B

Vi.Bi.

***T**HIS SMALL FACTORY IS NOT STRICTLY **A**RT **D**ECO because it was founded just after World War II, but it is included because it shows how the style endured. Like Lenci, Vi.Bi. was based in Turin, and it was directly inspired by that company's designs. It sought to perpetuate the fantasy models popular before the war, and this example is typical. Entitled "La Donna e la Piovra", it depicts a woman trying to escape an amorous octopus. The quality of the modelling is not quite up to Lenci standards, so the piece veers toward the kitsch.*

Height 13½in/34cm   £G

Wade

THE **W**ADE GROUP WAS FOR
*many years a conglomeration of
several small factories trading
under the Wade family name,
and did not unite as one
company until the
1950s. George
Wade & Sons was
formed in 1867, and
between 1927 and
1937 it produced a
series of 63 Art Deco
pottery figurines and wall
masks, designed by Jessica
Van Hallen, which are
unique in their use of
a cellulose finish.
The models were
fired, then dipped
in cellulose and, when dry, painted in colours.
Since the colours were not fired on to
the body they would often flake off, and the
cellulose itself deteriorated quickly and discoloured.
Because of this it is extremely unusual to find
examples, such as this figure entitled
"Springtime", which are in good condition.*
Height 8in/20cm £B

Wade's factory marks
are printed on the base with a
simple ink stamp.
"Wade" is in black, and the
leaping deer motif
is in red.

Louis Wain 1

The English artist and illustrator Louis Wain (1860–1939) spent his life producing comic pictures of cats and was a household name. In 1914 he began work on a series of cat mascots, including this version of the "Lucky Mascot Cat". The musical-style motifs on the body are "Meow Meow" notes and appear on several models. Although its whisker is broken, it is still highly prized and a collector's item.
Height 11in/28cm £G

Among the other known figures are the "Lucky Master Cat", "Lucky Knight-Errant Cat" and "Lucky Futurist Cat". They all have an impressed signature on the body and a cat's paw printed on the base.

Louis Wain II

OF ALL OF WAIN'S MODELS THESE ARE PERHAPS THE *most common. Top left is the "Lucky Haw-Haw Cat", its monocle and cigar identifying it with Lord Haw-Haw, who later made propaganda broadcasts for Germany during World War II. The top right model is unnamed; the one bottom left is the "Lucky Pig"; that on the right the "Lucky Bully Bulldog".*
Height 3½–4½in/9–11.5cm £D (all)

Wedgwood 1

Fairyland Lustre is synonymous with designer Daisy Makeig-Jones (1881–1945), who worked for Wedgwood from 1909 to 1931, producing numerous patterns incorporating fairies, elves and goblins. The designs were applied to porcelain pieces through a complicated – and not always successful – process of transfer printing, underglaze painting, overglaze lustre and printed gilding.

The "Bubbles II" design on this ginger jar (or Malfrey pot) shows the story of a nix, or waterman. He guarded the souls of the dead in an underwater palace, but a peasant released them all – shown here as black elves escaping in bubbles.

Height 9in/23cm £G

Wedgwood II

BEFORE FINALLY CONCENTRATING ON PATTERNS OF
*fairies and elves, Daisy Makeig-Jones produced other
fantasy designs. This pair of Dragon Lustre vases
copies 18th-century Chinese porcelain. They date
from the early 1920s and are one of her first designs.*
Height 10¼in/26cm   £C

The factory mark
is the famous Wedgwood
Portland Vase mark printed
in gilt on the base. On some
of the more elaborate
pieces Daisy Makeig-Jones
was known to include her
monogram in the
final gilding.

Wiener Werkstätte

FOUNDED BY JOSEF Hoffmann, Koloman Moser and Fritz Wärndorfer in Vienna, this association of workshops for artists and designers is seen as one of the great Modernist movements of the 20th century, guiding Europe away from Art Nouveau and toward Art Deco. It specialized in unique one-off designs, but was never successful commercially, even though examples can command thousands of pounds at auction and are on show in every major museum worldwide. Although the Wiener Werkstätte was active as early as 1903 – the Art Nouveau period – the earlier pieces looked forward to Art Deco, and many typically Art Deco items were produced until 1932.

THIS TIN-GLAZED RED TERRACOTTA GROUP IS TYPICAL. IT WAS designed by Susi Singer (1881–1965) in the 1920s, when the workshops were under the artistic directorship of Dagobert Pêche who encouraged less severe and more commercially appealing designs. The base is marked with the impressed entwined "W" mark, and with Singer's monogram.

Height 9in/23cm   £F

Frank Lloyd Wright

*Like the artists of the Wiener Werkstätte,
Frank Lloyd Wright (1869–1959), the American-
born architect and designer, was a Modernist,
although ironically he was committed to the ideals of
the Arts and Crafts Movement of 19th-century
Britain. His buildings, with their innovative use
of space and light, are considered some of the most
radical and avant-garde of their day.*

*As well as designing the buildings, Wright
was also responsible for the furniture and fittings
placed inside them. This service was produced
by the local porcelain firm Noritake for
Tokyo's Imperial Hotel which Wright designed in
1915. The pattern dates from c.1922 and is printed
and enamelled in colours, yet it is so modern
that it could easily be mistaken for a piece
of contemporary design.*

Diameter largest plate 8in/20cm   £E

Glossary

BASALT A fine hard black stoneware made by several of the Staffordshire potteries.

BONE CHINA A type of hard-paste porcelain made from a mixture of bone ash and kaolin.

CRACKLE A network of fine lines or cracks in the glaze caused by the body and the glaze contracting at different rates when fired.

EARTHENWARE Porous pottery fired at *c*.900–1,500°F (500–800°C). It must be glazed to be waterproof.

ENAMEL Form of decoration made from a mixture of powdered glass and pigmented metal oxides suspended in an oily medium. The oil burns off during firing, leaving a smooth finish.

FAIENCE French tin-glazed earthenware.

LUSTRE WARE Ceramics with a metallic or iridescent finish created by applying a metal oxide to the glaze and firing it in a reduced atmosphere, which converts the oxide back into a metal.

OVERGLAZE DECORATION Enamel colours painted or transfer printed on to a piece over the glaze and then refired at a relatively low temperature. Also known as on-glaze decoration.

PORCELAIN True, or hard-paste, porcelain is made from china clay and china stone and is white, translucent, strong and heat resistant.

POTTERY Another name for earthenware or stoneware.

THE POTTERIES Area in Staffordshire around the towns of Stoke-on-Trent, Burslem, Hanley, Tunstall, Longton and Fenton where many ceramics factories were based.

SGRAFFITO Design effect created by scratching the surface of a piece or scoring through unfired slip that has been applied to it.

SLIP Liquid clay used as a finish or for decoration.

STONEWARE A hard dense non-porous material made from clay fired to a point at which the individual grains of the clay fuse together.

TERRACOTTA Literally "baked earth", this low-fired unglazed earthenware is often rich in iron, so it turns a brick red colour when fired.

TIN GLAZE An opaque white glaze made from the basic lead glaze mixed with tin oxide.

TRANSFER PRINTING Method of applying decoration. A paper print of the design in metallic oxides is wrapped around the piece and burns off when fired.

TUBE LINING Decoration made by piping or trailing stiff slip on the surface of a piece.

UNDERGLAZE DECORATION Design applied to a piece before glazing and firing.

Index

Acknowledgments

All pictures courtesy of Christie's South Kensington
except for the f ollowing:
Christie's Images 14–15; Angelo Hornak 8–9;
Angelo Hornak, courtesy of Radio City Music Hall, New York 11;
Hulton Deutsch Collection 6–7.
Illustrators: **Carol Hill** (borders), **Debbie Hinks** (endpapers).